Women's Role in Kingdom Building

Women's Role in Kingdom Building

An inspiring, motivating, thought provoking book

Dr. Evelyn J. Williams-Reason

Copyright © 2022 by Dr. Evelyn J. Williams-Reason

All rights reserved. No part of this publication may be reproduced, distributed, or transmitted in any form or by any means, including photocopying, recording, or other electronic or mechanical methods, without the prior written permission of the author, except in the case of brief quotations embodied in critical reviews and certain other noncommercial uses permitted by copyright law.

Printed in the United States of America
ISBN 978-1-64133-661-1 (hc)
ISBN 978-1-64133-660-4 (sc)
ISBN 978-1-64133-662-8 (e)

Library of Congress Control Number: 2021921772

Religion/Spirituality
11.10.2021

MainSpring Books
5901 W. Century Blvd
Suite 750
Los Angeles, CA, US, 90045

www.mainspringbooks.com

Table of Contents

Abstract vii

Introduction 1

Chapter 1   Eve: Mother of All Who Have Lived
             (Genesis 3:20) 6

Chapter 2   Sarah: Unwavering Faith (Hebrews 11:11) 10

Chapter 3   Rahab: A Redeemed Life (Joshua 6:25) 16

Chapter 4   Naomi: Strong, God-fearing, and Influential
             (Ruth 1:8-9) 23

Chapter 5   Ruth: Loyal and Loving (Ruth 1:16) 30

Chapter 6   Esther: From Orphan to Queen
             (Esther 2:7, 17) 33

Chapter 7   Mary: Blessed and Highly Favored Among
             Women ((Luke 1:27-28) 38

Chapter 8   Mary Magdalene: Delivered From
             Demonic Oppression (Luke 8:2) 42

Chapter 9   Deborah: Prophetess, Judge, Warrior, Saved
             (Judges 4-5) 46

Chapter 10   Tamar: Daughter of A King, Yet Helpless
             (II Samuel 13:14) 49

Our Daily Prayer 53

Bibliography 55

ABSTRACT

According to the Word of God, the Bible, women were created by God, second to man ... from the side of man. When God created the heavens and the earth, He had a divine plan and purpose for everything that was created, from the starry skies to the bodies of water; from the flowers and trees, to the birds and the bees; from the creatures that fly to the ones that crawl.

Mankind was made in God's own image and placed in the Garden of Eden to rule the earth. The first man created by God, Adam, was made from the dust of the earth. The first woman created by God, Eve, was made from the side of Adam ... from his rib to be exact. This difference in the way God created the two of them was of great significance to God. He had rules for Adam and Eve in order for them to live peaceably in the Garden of Eden. They could have lived there forever had they only obeyed God's rules. From the moment of their disobedience, the rules and roles changed for everybody ... Adam, Eve, and yes, even the animals! No longer could the serpent walk on legs, and no longer could Adam and Eve live a life of ease. (Genesis, 3:9-19) As time went on, the earth was populated, and sin abounded on the earth. This human wickedness was unacceptable to God, and as usual, God had a plan.

He sent the great Flood upon the earth and the only humans saved were Noah and his family members. Even though the Flood did not wash away all the sin and iniquity of mankind, God still had a plan to save man from his evil deeds, and reconcile mankind back to Himself.

From God's covenant with Abraham, to the sacrificing of His Son, Jesus, on the cross, God has always had a plan. Now those of us who are here today, saved by God's grace, love and mercy, must witness for Him, and spread the 'Good News'. But how do WOMEN do that, with so much prejudice against them in the ministry and opposition in the pulpits at so many churches? What is God's plan for women in kingdom building? As a woman of God, I'm glad you asked!

Introduction

KINGDOM BUILDING IS THE PART WE as Christians play in persuading others to believe in Jesus Christ and accept Him as their Lord and Savior as He commanded in what is known as 'The Great Commission':

> "Go ye therefore, and teach all nations, baptizing them in the name of the Father, and of the Son, and of the Holy Ghost: Teaching them to observe all things whatsoever I have commanded you: and lo, I am with you always, even unto the end of the world." (Matthew 28: 19-20)

Originally, this commission was given to the eleven disciples (minus Judas Iscariot) after the resurrection of Jesus, in an appointed place in the mountains of Galilee. However, it is widely accepted today as being meant for everyone that believes in Jesus Christ. Mankind as a whole is commissioned to go, baptize, and teach.

The first thing we must grasp is that when the Word of God makes statements about "mankind", He is also including "women". In God, there is 'neither male nor female', which means that although there are apparent differences in the male and female structure and functions of the human body, in the spirit they are the same to God. He is not a respecter of persons. Therefore, in God's eyesight, the rules and regulations for living the holy life goes for men and women alike!

Throughout the Bible we see the differences that were made in biblical society between men and women. Women had to be silent in public and let their husbands do the talking. Women were forbidden to disagree or argue with the men in public. If a woman upset her husband for any reason, the man could get a divorce from her. However, a women could not initiate getting a divorce from the man no matter what the reasons were. Even when the bible refers to certain events such as the miracle of the "two fish and five loaves of bread feeding five thousand people", the women and children were not even counted in those 'people' that were mentioned!

To coin a popular phrase in the ministry, "WOMAN, THOU ART LOOSED!" . . . (Bishop T.D. Jakes, 1994) You are the head and NOT the tail, above, and NOT beneath! God has created all of us with a measure of natural abilities. This means that from the moment you were being formed in your mother's womb, you had special qualities that made you unique! You were fearfully and wonderfully made by God. (Psalms 139:13-16)

Just think, there have never been two people with the same fingerprints, so nobody can be you . . . but you! There is a special 'fingerprint of life' that was designed by God for all of us, which identifies the chosen pathway God has in His will for our lives. It is our job to discover the way we should go. Well, how do women go about finding their right path in kingdom building? Just like those fingerprints, no two women are exactly alike either, and it is because of the differences in the women that each woman must be careful NOT to try to be "just like" so-and-so! What gave one woman her niche to her success in ministry, may be another woman's downfall. While it is a wonderful thing to have someone to 'mentor' in your work of the ministry, always remember: You are *not them*, and they are *not you*!

Women of God, the word of God has the answer to every question you could ever think or ask. If not, God would not have said, "Ask, and it shall be given you; seek, and ye shall find; knock, and it shall be opened unto you." (Matthew 7:7) In your quest for your God given purpose in life, don't forget to ask GOD . . . seek GOD . . . and knock on GOD'S door every chance you get! After all, He is the author and finisher of our faith. God is the reason for everything, and everything and everybody was made for His purpose!

The ultimate goal of the entire universe is to show the glory of God! Everything comes from God alone, and everything lives only by His power. (Romans 11:36) The Lord has made all things for His own purposes, even the wicked for the day of evil. (Proverbs 16:4) Think on this: No matter what mankind thinks he has made, or invented, he will always need what God has already made, to do it. For example, if mankind says he makes great sky scraper buildings, he had to use God's trees for the wood, and God's minerals such as iron, silver, copper, ore, etc., for the foundation, framework and walls. To sweeten your coffee which comes from the earth (God's handiwork), you have to use His sugarcane, or his honey. Even if you just want a drink of water, who made the water? Everything comes from God's handiwork, the earth. Our food, shelter, clothing, even man comes from the dust of the earth. (Genesis 2:7)

So far, I have said all of that to impress three things upon the female species known as woman: It does not matter what you are going through, or have been through, remember:

(1) You are an intricate part of God's plan for mankind. He created you from the side of man, but woman, you are most definitely the head creation in charge of bearing the children, even bringing our Lord and Savior Jesus Christ into the world. No other species possess the ability to do what you do in that respect!

(2) Adam was made from dirt, but Eve was made from flesh and bone. This means that from the beginning, woman was wonderfully and fearfully made by God, in a special way belonging all to her. God was the original doctor, performing the first surgery ever made on His great creation, man. Even at that moment, God's plan for this beautiful creation,

woman, was for her to "bring forth His only begotten son, Jesus, wrap Him in swaddling clothes and lay Him in a manger!" How special can you call this? And finally,

(3) Woman of God, know WHO you are, and WHOSE you are!... You are a child of God, and you truly belong to Him. Need you be reminded that no weapon formed against you shall prosper? Always bear in mind that you were made for God, by God!

Now ladies, if you are still having a problem believing you are special to God, and have a direct part to play in kingdom building, then I suppose it is time to give you some more direct encouragement through examples from the Word of God.

Let me warn you, the examples that are given here may not be what you expect them to be. They are genuinely just ordinary people when it comes to their backgrounds and innate talents. In some cases, they may even be women with low-caste roles, and may not even have any particular distinction. However, they have been made to be extraordinary through their memorable, life changing encounters with the God of the universe. God has used these women for His divine purposes. He refined them like silver and gold, and because of the gracious works of God, they stand as reminders to us, of both our impotence and our importance . . . which greatly influences IF and HOW we reach our potential.

"For ye see your calling, brethren, how that not many wise men after the flesh, not many noble, *are called:* But God hath chosen the foolish things of the world to confound the wise; and God hath chosen the weak things of the world to confound the things which are mighty; and base things of the world, and things which are despised, hath God chosen, yea, and things which are not, to bring to nought things that are: That no flesh should glory in his presence. But of him are ye in Christ Jesus, who of God is made unto us wisdom, and righteousness, and sanctification, and redemption:

That, according as it is written, HE THAT GLORIETH, LET HIM GLORY IN THE LORD." (I Corinthians 1:26-31)

<u>The message for today is this:</u> As you emulate the faithfulness of these women, and learn to love the Savior whose work made them extraordinary, your life can also be extraordinary. If you examine the lives of these women, you will discover their struggles and doubts, their fears and failures, their faith and commitment. Through *their* stories, you will discover how God can impact the world through you!

EXAMPLE #1

<u>Eve</u>: Mother of All Who Have Lived (Genesis 3:20)

Eve, according to the Hebrew Bible, was the first woman created by God, and is an important figure in Judaism, Christianity, and Islam. Her husband was Adam, from whose rib God created her to be his companion. Perhaps you have heard the story, how the serpent had suggested to Eve that by eating the fruit from the Tree of Knowledge, it would not cause them to "surely die" at all. But it would make her and Adam wise like God, and would improve on the way God had made her. Eve believed the lies of the serpent, rather than the earlier instruction Adam had received from God.

Eve first, and then Adam, ate the forbidden fruit, and they became aware of their nakedness. (Genesis 3:6-7) After discovering their disobedience, God banished the couple from the garden in order to deny them access to the Tree of Life which would give them immortality. God cursed both the snake and the ground, obliging Adam to survive through agriculture "by the sweat of his brow." He told the woman that her childbirth pains would be greatly increased and that the man would rule over her. God set angels and a flaming sword at the East gate of the Garden of Eden to protect the tree of life from Adam, Eve, and their descendants. Wow! What a life for Eve!

Not much is known about Eve's growing up, or her family. Perhaps that's because she did not "grow up" nor have a family. We formulate our opinions about a person from these types of things, so what do we do or think about a person who had no childhood (parental guidance or upbringing), no education (did not go to school), no background (family, friends?). These are things we do NOT know.

However, what we DO know about Eve is that she was not *born*, but actually *created* by God Himself. Whatever she was inside, was given to her by God. After her creation, she was given to Adam for companionship. Whatever she needed to know about womanhood and a relationship was given to her by God. One day, she was left alone by God, and by the only other human on this earth. Had she ever even talked to any other living creature but Adam?

How was she equipped to carry on a conversation with the serpent? However, she did know enough to tell the serpent that God had told them (her and Adam) NOT to eat of the Tree of Knowledge . . . but she did not have the strength to resist the temptation that followed.

What would you do if you had been thrust into life as an adult, given to some man, tempted all alone by the devil, banished from the only home you had ever known, and then, your God told you that "in sorrow" you would "bring forth children"? . . . What the heck are 'children'?? . . . The plight of Eve in the beginning was not so good. The curses of Adam and the serpent impacted Eve's life greatly. The enmity (deep hatred and hostility) between her and the serpent, and then, having to follow her husband, Adam, into a lifetime of sweat and tilling the ground for food, where food had been readily available courtesy of God in the Garden of Eden was a curse to her too. When you add in *her* curse of having to bear children in sorrow, one has to wonder, how did she make it? And what about that part where "thy husband shall rule over thee" was given by God in His curse upon her? Woe was Eve!

After the birth of Seth, we don't hear another word about Eve. Apparently she must have "overcome" all her troubles and sorrows, because she went on to be fruitful and multiplied to replenish the earth with children, with Adam. Sure, like all of us, Eve sinned, tried to explain her way out of her sins (to God, no less), paid for those sins, and then got on with her life. There's no mistaking what Eve was called to do. Here is how she made it through: After all the havoc Adam, Eve, and the serpent caused upon the earth, following the birth of Enos (son of Seth), the bible says, ". . . then men began to call upon the name of the Lord." (Genesis 4:26)

Well, there you have it, ladies! Lesson from Eve is, after the sin, you can still take comfort and have hope. Repent, do what God tells you to do, and always call upon His name for all your needs. Oh yes, that part about Adam ruling over Eve, . . . Adam and Eve were two persons truly created equal, but they had a relationship whereby Adam was the head of that relationship as declared by God.(I Corinthians 11:11-12) Eve was created to be Adam's "help meet". (this is interpreted to be: a helper comparable to him, and a companion) (Genesis 2:18) In her part of the transgression, Eve "shall be saved in her childbearing, if they continue in faith, charity, and holiness with sobriety." (I Timothy 2:15)

Scripture does not give us any physical description of Eve. Her beauty, splendid as it must have been, is never mentioned or even implied. The focus of the biblical account of Eve is about her duty to her creator, and her role alongside her husband. Women today, those facts are significant, reminding us that the main and true distinguishing traits of "true feminine excellence" are not just superficial! Ask yourself these questions: "In what ways do you believe God is challenging you to 'adjust' your concept of feminine excellence?" . . .

"How do you believe a Christian woman should respond to 'being submissive' to her husband?" "What types of pressure do you feel, or have felt, to pursue equality with other people? . . . with men in general? . . . with men in the pulpit?" Just know, dear lady, that all kingdom building assignments do not end up in the pulpit!

In what ways are women to work with men to "have dominion over creation and subdue it"? Man and woman equally share God's image, and together exercise dominion over creation. They are under divine mandate of God to do those things, as well as "be fruitful and replenish the earth." These are things that neither one can do without the other.

We must work together to oversee the operation of God's creation!

Sarah: Unwavering Faith (Hebrews 11:11)

SARAH WAS THE WIFE OF ABRAHAM, being the granddaughter of his father Terah (Genesis 20:12). Her name was originally Sarai. According to Genesis 17:15, God changed her name to Sarah as part of a covenant with Yahweh after Hagar bore Abraham his son Ishmael. The Talmud identifies Sarai with Iscah, daughter of Abraham's deceased brother Haran. Sarah turns out to be Abraham's niece, and the sister of Lot and Milcah. (Genesis 11:29)

Sarai was so beautiful that all other persons seemed like apes in comparison. Even the hardships of her journey with Abraham did not affect her beauty. She was superior to Abraham in the gift of prophecy. She was the "crown" of her husband, and Abraham obeyed her words because he actually recognized and respected her superiority. She was the only woman whom God deemed worthy to be addressed by Him directly, all the other prophetesses receiving their revelations through angels. She was originally called "Sarai". Later she was called "Sarah" (princess), because she was the princess of her house and of her tribe.(The Hebrew name *Sarah* indicates a woman of high rank and is sometimes translated as "princess". It also means "lady.")

During their journey to Egypt, Abraham hid his wife Sarai in a chest so no one would see her. At the border, the chest had to pass through the hands of certain officials, who insisted on examining its contents in order to determine the amount of duty or tax they would have to pay. When it was opened a bright light proceeded from Sarai's beauty. From that moment on, every one of the officials wished to secure possession of her, each offering a higher sum than his rival. When brought before Pharaoh, Sarai lied and said that Abraham was her brother. King Abimelech sent for her and took Sarai unto himself, and thereupon bestowed upon her many presents and expensive gifts. As a token of his love for Sarai, the king also turned over his entire property to her, and gave her the land of Goshen as her hereditary possession. He gave her also his own daughter Hagar to serve Sarai as her slave. The king said, "It is better that my daughter should be a slave in the house of such a woman, than mistress in another house."

Sarai prayed to God to deliver her from the king's advances. So the Lord sent an angel, who struck the king whenever he attempted to touch her. The king was so bewildered by these blows that he spoke kindly to Sarai, who then confessed to him that she was Abraham's wife. Upon learning this, the king immediately ceased to annoy her. Then God came to King Abimelech in a dream and told him to restore Abraham and his wife Sarah, because Abraham was a prophet who would pray for him, that he would live. The king called Abraham unto him, and after conferring the truth about everything, he gave Abraham and Sarah sheep, oxen, servants, land to dwell upon, and a thousand pieces of silver. Then Abraham prayed unto God and King Abimelech was healed along with all of his household. (Genesis 20)

Abraham took Sarah and all that had been bestowed upon him by the king and settled in the land near Canaan, prospering. Sarah kept Hagar as her maidservant, and treated Hagar well, compelling women who came to visit her, to visit Hagar also. But Sarah was barren, and lamented constantly to Abraham about her not being able to have children. Then an idea came upon Sarah, that she would ask Abraham if he would take her maidservant, Hagar, to be his wife, and have a child through her for Sarah to raise. Abraham agreed, and took Hagar as his wife, and they conceived a son (whom they would call Ishmael). Hagar, after becoming pregnant by Abraham, began to act haughty with pride toward Sarai, throwing it in her face that she was pregnant by Abraham, where Sarah could not be. Sarah complained to Abraham, blaming him as though he was the cause of Hagar no longer respecting her. Abraham told Sarah that Hagar was *her* maidservant, and it was up to her to deal with Hagar about her attitude toward her, as she pleased. And indeed, Sarah dealt harshly with Hagar, making her life so miserable that she ran out into the desert, crying profusely. Then the voice of an angel of the Lord called out to Hagar, and asked her, "Where did you come from, and where will you go? Go back to your mistress Sarah, and submit to her authority. You are now with child, and will bare a son. His name shall be called Ishmael, for the Lord has heard your cries." Remarkably, Hagar did not argue with the voice, but she turned right around and started back home, with God's words penetrating her heart like a refreshing spring of cool water in the desert, calming her fears. God knows everything, even about the child in her womb who would be named Ishmael which means "God hears". (Genesis 16)

Order was restored to Abraham's household through the covenant made by God between the two of them. When the Lord told Abraham he would be the father of many nations, and he and Sarah would bare a son, and she would be the mother of many nations, Abraham burst out in laughter, wondering how was that going to happen, seeing that he was one hundred years old, and Sarah was ninety years old! Even Sarah laughed to herself when she overheard the Lord telling Abraham she would bare a son. Then the Lord said to Abraham, why did Sarah laugh and express her doubts? Is anything too hard for the Lord? Because Sarah was afraid, she lied and said "I did NOT laugh!" However, the Lord pressed Sarah and said to her, "Yes, you DID, laugh." (Genesis 17 and 18)

A year later, as God had spoken, Sarah gave birth to Isaac, whose name meant "laughter". Sarah exclaimed, "God has brought me laughter, and everyone who hears about this will laugh with me."

But Sarah's laughter ws short lived. After she gave birth to Isaac, the fireworks flared up once again between her and Hagar, the mother of Abraham's other son, Ishmael. This time, Sarah was not only angry with Hagar, but also she saw how Hagar's son mocked her son, Isaac on the day of the feast celebrating Isaac's being weaned.

Sarah told Abraham that Hagar and her son had to go. Although Abraham was grieved by this, God told him in essence, that Sarah was right, he must send Hagar and Ishmael away from their household, and that is what he did. You may think that was harsh of Abraham and Sarah to put Hagar and Ishmael out of their home, for them to just wander in the desert. It was heartwrenching, but God gave comfort to Abraham and also to Hagar regarding Ishmael. After all, that was still their son! God assured Abraham they would be fine, and his son would still be blessed and made a great nation.(Genesis 17:20)

Sarah has been depicted as the spiritual matriarch, and the ancient epitome of all faithful women. She spent the majority of her life believing for the fulfillment of a promise that surely did not immediately come to pass. Do you have any experiences of waiting many years for what you believe was a promise made to you by God? Was it thirty-five years or more? Did you give up because of the timing in your life, or your age, made it seem like it was never going to happen?

Sarah's story is a good example of God doing things *His* way . . . in *His* own time . . . and not necessarily in normal ways or the ways we might seek to employ. It is so important for us to trust God to use us, at any age, to reflect His omnipotence and the perfection of *His* timing. She was married to a God-fearing man and together they lived as nomads in a pagan society. On two occasions, she found herself in the harems of godless kings. As God-fearing people, we are frequently challenged today by godless people who are making godless decisions! . . . Sarah took some very bold steps in securing the position of her son Isaac as the promised heir to Abraham. In many ways today we are confronted to preserve the truth of God's Word so that it remains pure and uncompromised.

From the time she became Abraham's wife, Sarah desired one thing above all others and that was to have children. She was barren throughout her 'normal' childbearing years, and was obviously tortured by her childlessness. Every recorded episode of strife in her household was related to her frustrations about her own barrenness. It was eating her up inside, and she spent years in the grip of depression because of it. To a woman whose name means "princess" ... and to any woman who might have a "princess complex", accustomed to getting everything she wants out of life ... how difficult is it to face personal loss, failure, or a lack of achieving something so desperately desired?

"But Sarai was barren; she had no child". (Genesis 11:30) ... That one statement sums up everything the scripture has to say about the first sixty-five years of Sarah's life. What is something you have wanted all of your life and still have not received it? How is the Lord challenging YOU to deal with your unfulfilled desire? Sarah died at the age of 127 and was buried in Hebron. Between Isaac's birth and her own death were thirty-seven years, enough time to reflect on her life's adventure with God. Was she ashamed of her treatment of the ill-fated Hagar? Did she remember laughing when God told Abraham she would bear a child at the age of ninety? Did she have any idea she would one day be revered as the Mother of Israel, a true symbol of the promise of God? It is heartening to know that God accomplishes His purposes despite our frailties, our little faith, and our own self-reliance.

It is true, that Sarah's dogmatic attempts to help God keep His promise caused plenty of anguish. (Even today, the struggle between Israel and her Arab neighbors stems from the ancient strife between two women and the children they bore.) Still, despite her jealousy, anxiety, and skepticism about God's ability to keep His promises, there is no denying that Sarah was a risk-taker in the first degree, a woman who said goodbye to everything familiar to travel to a land about which she knew nothing; a real flesh-and-blood kind of lady who lived an adventure more strenuous than any fairy tale heroine . . . an adventure that began with a promise and ended with laughter.

Perhaps the Lord is challenging you to change the perspective you have on your own life. Have you tried to 'help' God do His work by implementing a plan of your own like Sarah did with Hagar? I believe she proved in a big way that God does not need our help, and we should wait on Him to reveal His plans to us in God's own time. Perhaps you have this 'great idea' you want to put in motion. Well, allow me to make a suggestion: Before you do anything . . . ask God about it first!

The plan that God had for Abraham, obviously held a key role in it for Sarah! Abraham could not have become the patriarch of a great nation if Sarah had not first become mother to his child. See how God's plan was working? Apparently no other woman could fulfill this plan. After all, Hagar was also the mother of Abraham's child, right? But Hagar was not working in God's plan.

You see, Woman of God, when God has a plan for YOU, it is only for YOU. Are you married? Is your husband deep into kingdom building on his own? What is he doing in the work of the ministry? How is he edifying the body of Jesus Christ? Could it be that while you are trying to think 'outside the box' for your calling in kingdom building, you just might fit right into God's plan for you by working along side your husband, oh dear 'help meet' that you were originally created by God to be! . . . Help him fulfill *his* destiny, while fulfilling *your* calling. Think about it . . . Now pray and ask God about it!

Rahab: A Redeemed Life (Joshua 6:25)

RAHAB IS ONE OF THE MOST amazing and thought provoking women of the Old Testament. She was a prostitute who not only has earned unique praises for her faith, but also a place in the lineage of Jesus Christ. Certainly the faith this one woman revealed demonstrates the potential that we all have; yet, she also reminds us to not judge. After all, how many of us would expect a great act of faith from what we call today, a 'hooker'? How many of us would not only have walked on by her house, but also crossed to the other side of the street so as not to be contaminated. Yet, God blessed this woman by putting her in the lineage of Jesus Christ. God's blessings come in surprising packages.

We first meet Rahab in the book of Joshua, Chapter 2, where Joshua, the son of Nun sent two men secretly from the city of Shittim as spies and told them, 'Go, view the land, especially Jericho.' So they went, and entered the house of a prostitute whose name was Rahab and they spent the night there.'

Here we learn three things about Rahab: (1) She is a prostitute, (2) She lives in Jericho, and (3) that spies go to a prostitute's house while on the job. There are many "Bible Story" pictures showing Rahab demurely dressed, standing in the foyer of a cheery little cottage, a cozy fire warming the room and sweet little flowers to enliven the room. Unfortunately, from what we know of prostitution realities back then and now, that scene is misleading. Instead, we should visualize a small cramped area, where places of dirty outcasts live. This isn't a woman dressed in Sunday best, but for a 'Saturday night special'. Only by facing the harsh, true reality of Rahab's life, can we truly learn from her. Her society would have rejected her. Her career would have exposed her to dirty, possibly diseased men who sought to use her for one purpose only.

However, Rahab's story doesn't end here, and we have other questions to consider. Why did these men go to a prostitute's house when they were supposed to be viewing the land? What exactly could they spy on there? The Bible doesn't indicate there were others in the house to "eavesdrop on", so why were they there? The Bible doesn't tell us, though the most obvious answer is usually dismissed. Sometimes we like to think this was just an inn, and the two men were just renting a room. This wasn't an inn, though we could possibly believe they were just renting a room. While that is an interesting question, the Bible really has something to teach us in this story.

The king of Jericho was told, 'Some Israelites have come here tonight to search out the land.' Then the king of Jericho sent orders to Rahab, 'Bring out the men who have come to you, who entered your house, for they have come only to search out the whole land.' But the woman took the two men and hid them. Then she said, 'True, the men came to me, but I did not know where they came from. And when it was time to close the gate at dark, the men went out. Where the men went I do not know. Pursue them quickly, for you can overtake them. (Joshua 2:2-7) She had, however, brought them up to the roof and hidden them with the stalks of flax that she had laid out on the roof.

Rahab betrayed her own people. The Israelites were seeking to take Jericho, and Rahab had the opportunity to stop them, but she didn't. Rahab found herself in a position many teachers claim never happens. She had to decide between God's plan and the plans of earthly authority. Yet, this section reminds us of something else, as well. We tend to expect women to be either entirely good, or entirely bad. The church accepts the follies of man, while either denying women have follies, or seeing the follies of women as a sign of ungodliness. Much like Jacob and his divining rod, Rahab proves she is a cracked vessel even as she operates in great faith. She steps out in faith . . . and lies to do it! Certainly the Lord is not instructing us in situational ethics, but rather, the Word demonstrates that women are human too. They are capable of great acts of faith, just like men. Equally, women are capable of great acts of error, just like men.

This passage also offers an interesting mirror to other more famous "intruder" stories in the Bible. In Genesis, Lot offers his two daughters for the sexual use of a crowd in place of his visitors. Later in Judges the Levite will thrust his wife out the door into the hands of a rapine mob. Yet, when Rahab, a woman, a lowly prostitute, faces this same challenge, she responds differently. When the crowd comes to her door, she uses her brain to solve the problem; the men in similar stories resort to sacrificing the "least of these" in their midst. I have often wondered how many times I've been Lot instead of Rahab. How many times have I sacrificed the ones I should have protected? . . . How about you?

Before the men went to sleep, she came up to them on the roof and said to them, 'I know that the Lord has given you the land, and that dread of you has fallen on us, and that all the inhabitants of the land melt in fear before you. For we have heard how the Lord dried up the water of the Red Sea before you when you came out of Egypt, and what you did to the two kings of the Amorites that were beyond the Jordan, to Sihon and Og, whom you utterly destroyed. As soon as we heard it, there was no courage left in any of us because of you. The Lord your God is indeed God in heaven above and on earth below.' (Joshua 2:8-11)

Finally, we learn why Rahab betrayed her people. She heard what the Lord had done, and she believed. Too many times we hear what the Lord has done and refuse to believe, or worse, we believe but refuse to act on that belief. Rahab believed and acted, even though acting put her life on the line. We often talk about 'stepping out in faith', but many times that step has little meaning because the drop is small. An abyss awaited Rahab with her first step. The life of a traitor would truly be short, especially the life of a traitorous harlot like Rahab.

Rahab said to the men, 'Now then, since I have dealt kindly with you, swear to me by the Lord that you in turn will deal kindly with my family. Give me a sign of good faith that you will spare my father and mother, my brothers and sisters, and all who belong to them, and deliver our lives from death.' (Joshua 2:12-13)

Now Rahab has faith not only in what God has done, and can do, but in faith of what He will do. She has faith that He will spare her family. This verse also presents a mystery: Why is Rahab a prostitute if she has not only a father, but brothers to help provide for her? The Bible doesn't tell us. Yet, if we think about Rahab's life, her faith shines even brighter. She is an outcast, a prostitute. Rejected by society, she still trusts that the Lord will not reject her. Abandoned by her family (we assume) to a life of prostitution, she trusts that the Lord will not abandon her.

The men said to her, 'Our life for yours! If you do not tell this business of ours, then we will deal kindly and faithfully with you when the Lord gives us the land.' Then she let them down by a rope through the window, for her house was on the outer side of the city wall and she resided within the wall itself. Rahab said to them, 'Go toward the hill country, so that the pursuers may not come upon you. Hide yourselves there three days, until the pursuers have returned; then afterward you may go your way.' The men said to her, 'We will be released from this oath that you have made us swear to you, if we invade the land and you do not tie this crimson cord in the window through which you let us down, and you do not gather into your house your father and mother, your brothers, and all your family. If any of you go out of the doors of your house into the street; they shall be responsible for their own death and we shall be innocent; but if a hand is laid upon any who are with you in the house, we shall bear the responsibility for their death. But if you tell this business of ours, then we shall be released from this oath that you made us swear to you.' She said, 'According to your words, so be it.' She sent them away and they left.

By this time, Rahab has already expressed faith: she acknowledged God, and knew He could and would act in her life. However, there was more to be done. Faith alone isn't good enough, although we Protestants like to think so. Faith must produce action. As the Book of James tells us, "faith without works is dead." The two spies made it very clear to Rahab in their explanation that she must act, she must not betray them, and she must put the scarlet cord in the window. Failure to act, despite her claim of faith, would result in her destruction. That is why Rahab tied the crimson cord in the window, and faithfully waited for the results. (Joshua 2:14-21)

The city and all that was in it would be devoted to the Lord for destruction. Only Rahab the prostitute and all who were with her in her house will live because she hid the messengers that were sent. Rahab's faith and action proved to save not only herself but her entire family.

We have this same opportunity today, in many forms. Stepping out in faith can never be easy. If it were, it wouldn't be faith. But by walking in faith we open the door for the Holy Spirit to work not only in our lives, but in the lives of our loved ones.

Joshua said to the two men who had spied out the land, 'Go into the prostitute's house, and bring the woman out of it and all who belong to her, as you swore to her.' So the young men who had been spies went in and brought Rahab out, along with her father, her mother, her brothers and all who belonged to her. They brought all her kindred out and set them outside the camp of Israel. They burned down the city, and everything in it; only the silver and gold, and the vessels of bronze and iron, they put into the treasury of the house of the Lord. But Rahab the prostitute, her family, and all who belonged to her, were spared by Joshua. (Joshua 6:17-25)

Rahab's family has lived in Israel ever since, because she hid the messengers whom Joshua sent to spy out Jericho. This first New Testament reference to Rahab shows just how richly God blessed Rahab. Matthew 1:5 reads: "and Salmon the father of Boaz by Rahab, and Boaz the father of Obed by Ruth, and Obed the father of Jesse". This list of names is part of the Christ's genealogy. Chroniclers didn't need to include women in a genealogy, but the author of Matthew's Gospel included four such women. He lists Tamar, Rahab, Ruth and Bathsheba. Of these four, only Bathsheba was Jewish. However, all four are united by another factor. Their biblical stories involved sexual scandal. Tamar played the harlot to gain a son; Rahab, of course, was a prostitute; Ruth initiated a seduction; and Bathsheba was, for a time, mistress to the king. Not exactly the line-up we expect. No mention of Sarah or Rebekah or Leah or Rachel. Interestingly, this verse also gives us a glimpse into Rahab's fate with her chosen people. We know from Ruth's story that Boaz was a wealthy and prominent man in his community. We also know he was an honorable man. Rahab apparently played a role in Boaz's father's life. Did this prostitute become the wife of a wealthy community leader, as some women went from the depths of prostitution to nobility in the 1700s?

Hebrews 11:31 says:

> "By faith Rahab the prostitute did not perish with those who were disobedient, because she had received the spies in peace."

James 2:24-26 says:

> "You see that a person is justified by works and not by faith alone. Likewise, was not Rahab the prostitute also justified by works when she welcomed the messengers and sent them out by another road?

For just as the body without the spirit is dead, so faith without works is also dead."

James reminds us that faith can't be just words . . . or even sincere emotion. If we say we have faith and do nothing based on that faith, then our faith is worthless. For us Protestants this seems to contradict "justification by faith"; however, in my view, it does not. To me, faith and works have the same relationship as our love of God and our love of our brothers and sisters. I can 'think' I love God with all my heart, but if I do not actually 'love' my brothers and sisters, then I do not truly love God. Yet when I love God, by the very fact of loving God, I love my brothers and sisters.

The story of Rahab reveals to us, again, God's willingness to use the "less than perfect", the outcast, what we might see as the unsuitable, to accomplish God's holy purposes! God does not wait for us to become spotlessly clean or totally mature in our faith in order to use us in kingdom building. Instead, he takes ordinary, willing people and accomplishes the extraordinary, both in their lives, and in the lives of those around them.

As God did with Rahab, He promises to use us in His kingdom building, and through those experiences, He will perfect us.

EXAMPLE #4

Naomi: Strong, God-fearing, and Influential (Ruth 1:8-9)

NAOMI: "PLEASANT; AGREEABLE; MY SWEET" . . . A standard Hebrew name. Naomi is Ruth's mother-in-law in the Old Testament Book of Ruth. Located in the Book of Ruth are the struggles of Naomi and Ruth for survival in a patriarchal environment. Though the book takes its name from the younger woman, Ruth, the older one, Naomi, is the dominant character. Naomi's plight begins the saga, and her plan brings it to a resolution.

Chapter one opens with a "famine in the land," (Bethlehemjudah was that land) that sends a Judean family across the Jordan to Moab, a foreign land. The way that family was introduced in the Book of Ruth, the writer made it quite plain how the women were thought of in those "days when the judges ruled." The name of the man is Elimelech. Naomi was "his wife," and their children are "his" two sons (emphasis added). But *after* the death of Elimelech, the whole situation changed. He became Naomi's husband, and she is left with "her" two sons. (emphasis added). The two sons married Moabite women, Orpah and Ruth, and they all dwelled in the country of Moab for about ten years. Then, Mahlon and Chilion, Naomi's sons not only died, but they both died without progeny. How disheartened Naomi was, dealing with tragic death, again! From wife to widow, from mother of two children to childless, this woman's heart had been ripped right out of her chest. (Ruth 1:1-5)

Can you imagine Naomi trying to remain focused on living, trying to remember what it felt like to be a whole person? What would it take for her to just feel secure again? Laugh again? Although she could see for miles front her point on the road that led from Moab to Judah, she could see nothing at all of a future for herself. What more could be taken from her at this point? Moses had been buried somewhere in these mountains, but his people and hers had moved west into Canaan centuries ago. Is it possible she would be left behind, to never see her kinsmen again? Was God so displeased with her? Ten years ago she and Elimelech had been so happy living in Bethlehem. But now, in the city whose name meant "house of bread", suddenly had nothing to eat. Plenty of women had lost their husbands, but Naomi had suffered the worst grief a mother could endure . . . outliving her own children. And, alas, no grandchildren had been conceived to neither console her nor carry on the family name. (Ruth 1:1-5)

Upon hearing that the Lord has restored food to Judah, Naomi's thoughts turned to making the journey to return home. Ruth and Orpah, her daughters-in-law, were the only kin she had in Moab. Loving them from the depths of her heart, she felt their widowhood grief as much as she had felt her own grief. Together they had cried and comforted each other, finally deciding to leave Moab for Bethlehem for good. But once they got on the road, Naomi had misgivings that outweighed her need for companionship. It was not right for these young women to forsake their families and friends for such a highly uncertain future. What chance would they have in Bethlehem, as widows and strangers to the land? She told each of her daughters-in-law, "Return to your own mother's house, and may the Lord show kindness to you as you have shown to your dead husbands and to me. May the Lord grant each of you true rest in the home of another husband." Then Naomi kissed them, and they cried all the more! (Ruth 1:6-9)

Here we see the kind, loving, and sympathetic mother-in-law attributed to Naomi. She was still mourning the deaths of her husband, and both her sons. She saw herself as a 'nobody', with nothing left in life to give. She still could not see a future for herself, so how could she drag her daughters-in-law into the same useless and uncertain future as she was destined to live? She loved them too much to allow that to happen.

Nonetheless, both Ruth and Orpah insisted they wanted to stay with Naomi and return with her to her people's homeland. Strikingly, the basis on which Naomi invokes divine intervention is the loyalty that Orpah and Ruth have already shown her family. She lifts up these two female foreigners as models for what God 'ought' to do. Then she spells out the content of life for a woman who lives in a man's world, which is to find a home, "each of you in the house of your husband". Naomi shapes a theology that paradoxically resists yet serves patriarchy. Yet, to put it in our terms today, Naomi knew 'what's up' with the differences between men and women, and the expectations of their roles back then.

When the daughters-in-law insist upon returning with her, Naomi sought to dissuade them, using rhetorical questions, and resorting to sound reasoning: She has no sons now in her womb to provide them with husbands, and even if she did, why would these two young women wait for them to grow up? By then, the women would be too old! Describing her situation, Naomi concludes that the Lord has turned against her. It grieved her to say so, but the God whom she had hoped would show mercy to her daughters-in-law had shown hostility toward her, and put up His hand against her. Once more, her daughters-in-law "lifted up their voices and wept again." Orpah kissed her mother-in-law goodbye. However, that Ruth clung all the more as Naomi continued to try to sway her to return to her own people with Orpah. Alas, with all of her words of protest, Naomi could only convinces Orpah to return to her own mother. (Ruth 1:10-15)

Having made up her mind, and refusing to be dissuaded, Ruth was determined that she would accompany Naomi to Bethlehem. She fiercely leaned toward her mother-in-law and declared to her.

"Don't even think about trying to keep me from going to Bethlehem with you. I will not let you make this journey alone. Where you go, I will go; where you stay, I will stay. Your people shall be my people, and your God, my God!" Ruth went on to say, "Where you die, that's where I will die and be buried. If the Lord says the same, only death will be able to part you and me!" (Ruth 1:16-17)

Wow! How heavy is that? Can you influence someone in your life to denounce their family, their homeland, their roots, AND their God/god??!! Now we see the affects that a strong, loving God fearing character like Naomi, could have on a person, and just how influential she truly, truly was with Ruth.

When Naomi saw that Ruth could not be dissuaded from going to Bethlehem with her, she stopped speaking to Ruth. I believe she also realized that her old woman stubbornness was no match for the younger woman's love for her, and just didn't know what else to say. So the two continued on their journey, and when they arrived in Bethlehem, it was in the beginning of the barley harvest. The women of the town focused attention upon Naomi, asking, "Is this Naomi?" Referring to the death of her husband, Elimelech and her two sons, Mahlon and Chilion, Naomi answered them, saying, " I left home full, and the Lord has brought me home again, and empty! Don't call me 'Naomi' (which means 'pleasant') but instead, call me 'Mara' (which means 'bitter'), for the Almighty has dealt very bitterly with me." (Ruth 1:18-22)

Naomi could not see past her suffering and began to actually become bitter. Like many of us, she may have felt that her tragedies in life were punishment for her sins. Had she known the blessings yet in store for her, she might not have felt so hopeless. Instead, she might have compared herself to the tree that Job so graciously describes:

> "There is hope for a tree: If it is cut down, I will
> sprout again, and its new shoots will not fail. Its
> roots may grow old in the ground, and its stump die

in the soil, but yet, at the mere scent of water it will bud and put forth shoots like a plant." (Job 14:7-9)

Although Naomi did not know it, the scent of water was in the air, and her life was about to begin again; her life was still unfolding. God's faithfulness to restore an empty life to fullness, is revealed more in this story of Naomi than in any other biblical account.

Naomi's prominence links her to a wealthy kinsman named Boaz. Meanwhile, Naomi grants Ruth permission to go into the fields so she can glean ears of corn wherever she is received. She happened to light on a part of the field belonging to Boaz, who was kin to Elimelech, Naomi's deceased husband. Ruth found favor with the reapers, then with Boaz, and was allowed to glean off Boaz's fields as long as she was in Bethlehem. He even let Ruth dine with him and his household. When they finished eating, they went back into the fields to reap. Boaz told his servants to leave some extra sheaves for Ruth to glean, knowing that she was gathering food to feed her mother-in-law, Naomi. (Ruth 2:1-17)

In the evening Ruth returns to Naomi, who initiates conversation as they ate, asking about how she had spent her day. After hearing about the events of Ruth's day, Naomi utters words of blessing for the first time since they had left Moab. They talked about this man, as yet unidentified for her, who helped Ruth. Upon learning that the man was Boaz, Naomi adds the name of the Lord to her blessing and so invokes the God whom she has earlier faulted as the giver of bitterness. She tells Ruth that Boaz is a very close relative of theirs. Naomi is changing her attitude to one of gratitude. Ruth continued to glean in Boaz's field until the end of harvest, and dwelt with her mother-in-law and took care of her. (Ruth 2:18-23)

Still being the enterprising woman she was, and not waiting for matters to take their course or for God to intervene, Naomi plans to secure Boaz as husband for Ruth. In seeking security through marriage, her plan fits the standards of patriarchy, but it departs from them in proposing a dangerous scheme. Naomi told her "daughter" to dress in fine clothes and visit Boaz in secret at the threshing floor. There she will ask him to make good on his prayer for her blessing. The plan succeeds. From being the receiver of calamity, she has become the agent of change and challenge.

Naomi does not speak again after the third chapter; her work is basically finished. Nevertheless, she figures prominently in the lives of Ruth and Boaz. Boaz depicts Naomi as the owner of property, an heiress. The women of Bethlehem invoke God's blessing upon Naomi through Ruth and the grandchild Ruth bears for her. The writer reports that Naomi embraces the child and becomes his nurse. And at the end, the women even declare that the child has been born to Naomi. (Ruth 4)

Feminist assessments of Naomi diverge widely, depending often upon the cultural, social, ideological, and experiential biases of readers. As you read the following contrasting opinions about Naomi, decide which you see as true . . . or not true:

Naomi is a cipher for male values that find fulfillment for women in marriage and children. In contrast to the loss of status for childless widows in patriarchy, Naomi achieves importance as a mother-in-law and an independent character.

- Naomi is an overbearing, interfering, and domineering mother-in-law.
- Naomi is a caring, gracious, and altruistic mother-in-law.
- Naomi the Judean rejects Ruth (and Orpah) because she is a Moabite.
- Naomi embraces Ruth the Moabite within the family of Judah.
- Naomi and Ruth are rivals, with Naomi eventually achieving the greater prestige.
- Naomi and Ruth are friends, indeed sister like, each seeking the good of the other in a world over which they have little control.
- Naomi schemes, connives, and manipulates.

- Naomi plans, reflects, and executes.
- Naomi is an embittered old woman who denounces God for her troubles but fails to thank the deity when she recovers.
- Naomi is a profound figure of faith that experiences God as enemy but then wrestles a blessing from adversity.

All such disparate judgments affirm Naomi's commanding presence (although it may be ambiguous) in one of the few biblical stories focused on women. Suffering a threefold tragedy, Naomi refused to hide her sorrow or bitterness. What are you trying to hide that is a major concern in your life? Believing in God's sovereignty, Naomi even attributed her suffering to His will. She finally learned that her fixation on her circumstances, both past and present, led to a feeling of hopelessness. Once Naomi decided to be true to whom she really was, a strong, God fearing woman who possessed the ability to influence many people, her life took a significant change.

Do you know *who* you are? . . . Do you know *whose* you are?

EXAMPLE #5

<u>Ruth</u>: Loyal and Loving (Ruth 1:16)

RUTH IS A COMMON FEMALE GIVEN name. It comes from Ruth the Moabite in the Bible, and is Hebrew for "compassion". Ruth is the great-grandmother of David and, according to the Christian tradition, an ancestor of Jesus Christ. The Book of Ruth is one of the only two books of the Bible which are named after a woman. The other one is The Book of Esther, which we will address later.

During the time of the Judges when there was a famine, an Israelite family from Bethlehem, Elimelech, his wife Naomi, and their sons Mahlon and Chilion, migrate to the nearby country of Moab. Elimelech dies, and the sons marry two Moabite women: Mahlon marries Ruth and Chilion marries Orpah. The two sons of Naomi then die themselves. Naomi decides to return to Bethlehem. She told her daughters-in-law to return to their own mothers, and remarry. Orpah reluctantly leaves; however, Ruth boldly protests, saying, "Entreat me not to leave you, or to turn back from following you; For wherever you go, I will go; And wherever you lodge, I will lodge; Your people shall be my people, and your God, my God. Where you die, I will die, and there will I be buried. The LORD does so to me, and more also, if anything but death parts you and me." (Ruth 1:16–17)

So, Naomi and Ruth returned to Bethlehem. It is the time of the barley harvest, and in order to support her mother-in-law and herself, Ruth went to the fields to glean. The field she chose to glean on belonged to a man named Boaz, who was kin to Elimelech, Naomi's deceased husband. (Was this just a coincidence? Or, was this an example of things working together for the good . . . you know!?)

Later on, Boaz entered the fields, greeted the reapers who were working there, and blessed them. When Boaz noticed Ruth, he inquired of the reapers, "Whose damsel is this?" The servant who was over the reapers identifies her to him by saying, "She is the Moabite damsel who came back with Naomi out of the country of Moab. She asked if she could glean after the reapers and I granted her permission to do so." Now Ruth found favor in the field of Boaz and he said to Ruth, "Don't go into any other field to glean, but stay here in my fields close to my maidens, reaping after them only where they have reaped. I have instructed the young men that they are not to touch thee. When you are thirsty, drink from the vessels which the young men have drawn water." (Ruth 2:1-9)

Ruth was so overtaken, that she fell on her face before Boaz and asked him, "Why have I found such grace in your eyesight, that you take interest in me, a stranger to you?" And Boaz answered her, "It has been fully revealed to me all that you have done for your mother-in-law since the death of your husband, and how you left your own parents and homeland to be with Naomi in this foreign land. Surely the Lord God of Israel whom you have come to trust, rewards your work." (Ruth 2:10-12)

Let's pause right there! Try to truly grasp what Boaz just said unto Ruth. Surely, the same thing happens to us when we dare to trust in the Lord God . . . He rewards our work! If we could truly, totally trust in God, then peace, joy and prosperity would enter our lives with such an impact! We would be more equipped to minister to others about the goodness of Jesus Christ. We could more easily recognize God's intentions for our part in kingdom building! . . . Oh yes, peace of mind helps us to be able to focus and think better every time!

After Ruth returns to Naomi, they have conversation about all the events of Ruth's day in Boaz's field. Naomi is awakening in her spirit now, as she began to see how she can effectively bring Boaz and Ruth together in matrimony, legally as the laws dictated.

Boaz is a close relative of Naomi's husband's family. He is therefore obliged by the Levirate law to marry Mahlon's widow, Ruth, in order to carry on his family line. Naomi sends Ruth to the threshing floor at night and tells her to "uncover the feet" of the sleeping Boaz. Ruth does so, Boaz awakes, and Ruth reminds him that he is "the one with the right to redeem." Boaz states he is willing to "redeem" Ruth via marriage, but informs Ruth that there is another male relative who has the first right of redemption.

The next morning, Boaz discussed the issue with the other male relative before the town elders. The other male relative was unwilling to jeopardize the inheritance of his own estate by marrying Ruth, so he relinquished his right of redemption, thus allowing Boaz to marry Ruth. They transferred the property and redeemed it by taking off a shoe and handing over the shoe. Boaz and Ruth got married and had a son named Obed. (Ruth 4:7-18)

Everything Ruth did was done out of love for her mother-in-law, and for the love of Naomi's God. She made a promise on the road to Bethlehem, which she was determined to keep. She had no way of knowing that her way of blessing Naomi would eventually become a blessing in her own life. That's just the "divine irony" of our God, who delights so much in seeing us love and bless others, that He turns that love and blessing back on us in double, sometimes 'fourfold' measure. Did it not all lead to another person being born in the lineage of our Lord and Savior Jesus Christ?

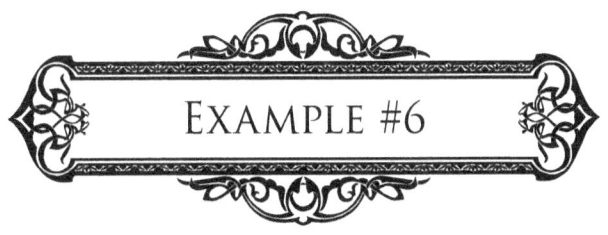

Esther: From Orphan to Queen (Esther 2:7, 17)

According to the Esther 2:7, Esther was originally named "Hadassah". Hadassah means "myrtle" in Hebrew. It has been conjectured that the name Esther is derived from a reconstructed Median word "astra" also meaning myrtle. In the Talmud Esther is compared to the "morning star", and is considered the subject of Psalm 22 because its introduction is a "song for the morning star." Esther can also be understood to mean "hidden" in Hebrew, where it is said that Esther hid her nationality and lineage as Mordecai had advised. Because the methods and aims of God are believed to be similarly hidden, "The Book of Esther" in Hebrew can be understood as "The Book of Hiddenness," representing God's hiddenness in the story.

It's easy to dismiss Queen Esther as the lucky orphan girl who won the heart of the king. But in reality, she was a young woman with a tragic background and dangerous secret that could cost her life and her family's. She was married to a king who destroyed peoples' lives on a whim and had a history of killing people close to him. Worse still, the king's favorite counselor and chief advisor was a mortal enemy of Esther's family. Esther had to keep a low profile, keeping her secret, hoping he wouldn't make the connection. For Esther, life was unfair. But her story brings a message of hope to all who face trouble by showing how God works even through the fears and dangers. There are happy endings in perilous times!

The Book of Esther tells a story of palace intrigue and genocide which was thwarted by a Jewish queen of Persia. The book began with a feast organized by Ahasuerus, initially for his court and dignitaries and afterwards for all inhabitants of Shushan. He ordered his wife Vashti to display her beauty before the guests. She refused. Ahasuerus removed her as queen, then ordered all "beautiful young girls" to be presented to him, so he could choose a new queen to replace Vashti. One of those would be Esther, who had no parents and was being fostered by her cousin, Mordechai. She found favor in the king's eyes, and was made his new wife. Esther did not reveal that she was Jewish. (Esther 1, 2:1-20)

Shortly afterwards, Mordechai discovered a plot by courtiers Bigthan and Teresh to assassinate King Ahasuerus. They are apprehended and hung, and Mordechai's service to the king was recorded. Ahasuerus appoints Haman as his prime minister. Mordechai, who sits at the palace gates, falls into Haman's disfavor as he refuses to bow down to him. Having found out that Mordechai is Jewish, Haman plans to kill not just Mordechai but *all* the Jews in the empire. He persuaded Ahasuerus to issue a commandment and decree to execute this plan, against payment of ten thousand talents of silver, and he cast lots to choose the date on which to do this—the thirteenth of the month of Adar. (Esther 2:1-23, 3:1-15)

When Mordechai finds out about the plans he rent his clothes and put on sackcloth with ashes; then went out into the middle of the city crying bitterly. In every province, when the Jews heard the King's commandment and decree, there was weeping, wailing, fasting, and many were in sackcloth and ashes. Then Mordechai informed Esther what has happened and tells her to intercede with the King. She was afraid to break the law and go to the King without being summoned. This action could incur the death penalty. Mordechai told her that she *must* do it to save their people, the Jews. So Esther requested of Mordechai, "Gather all the Jews present in the city of Shushan and have them fast and pray with me, neither eating nor drinking for three days, night and day. On the third day I will go in unto the King, and if I perish, I perish!" (Esther 4:1-17)

So, on the third day, Queen Esther put on her royal apparel, and went out and stood in the inner court of the King's house. As the King sat upon his royal throne, he beheld the beauty of Esther standing in the court, and he stretched out his scepter to her which showed that she had found favor with him and was not to be punished. Esther invited the King to a feast in the company of Haman. During the feast, she asked them to attend another feast the next evening. Meanwhile, Haman was again offended by Mordechai and his lack of respect for him. When Haman went home, he told his wife and friends all about his honor of being in the presence of both the King and Queen, and all the other accolades bestowed upon him. Then he said, "Yet all of this avails me nothing, as long as I see Mordecai the Jew sitting at the King's gate." His wife, Zeresh, and his friends suggested that he "build a gallows fifty cubits high, and speak with the King tomorrow about hanging Mordecai on it. Then go into the banquet merrily with the King." That suggestion pleased Haman, so he caused the gallows to be made. (Esther 5:1-14)

That night, King Ahasuerus suffered from insomnia, so he ordered the court's book of records of the chronicles be brought unto him and read to him to help him sleep. He learned of the services rendered by Mordechai in the previous plot against his life, and was told that Mordechai had never received any recognition for saving the king's life. Just then, Haman appeared in the court, and King Ahasuerus told his servants to let him come in. When he walks in, immediately the King asks Haman, "What should be done for the man that the King delights to honor?" Thinking that the man that the king wishes to honor is himself, Haman says, "The man should be dressed in the king's royal robe, his royal crown on his head, and led around on the king's royal horse, while a herald proclaims: "See how the king honors a man he wishes to reward!" Then, to his horror, the King instructs Haman to do all of what he had suggested, unto Mordechai. So Haman did as the King ordered, and when Mordecai returned back to the King's gate, Haman hasted back to his own house, mourning, with his head covered. Then he told his wife Zeresh, and all his friends about everything that had happened to him. Then his wise men and his wife told Haman, "If Mordecai is indeed the seed of the Jews, before whom you have begun to fall, then you will not prevail against him, and you will surely fall before him." . . . And while they were yet speaking to Haman, the King's servants came to take him to the banquet that Esther had prepared. (Esther 6:1-14)

Later that evening, King Ahasuerus and Haman attended Esther's second banquet, at which she revealed that she was Jewish and that Haman was planning to exterminate her people, including her. Overcome by rage, Ahasuerus left the room and went into the palace garden. Meanwhile, Haman stayed behind and as he was begging Esther for his life, he fell upon the bed where Esther was sitting. The King came back in at that very moment and thought Haman was assaulting the Queen! That made him even angrier than he was before he left the room. A servant then reminded the King of the fifty cubits high gallows that Haman had built for Mordecai, and in his rage, the King ordered Haman be hung on the gallows that had been prepared for Mordechai. (Esther 7:1-10)

On that same day, King Ahasuerus gave the lavish house of Haman unto Esther. And Mordecai came before the King, as Esther had told the King of the kinship between them. The King took off his ring which he had taken from Haman, and gave it to Mordecai. The King's commandment and decree against the Jews could not be annulled, but the King did make another decree, allowing the Jews to defend themselves during the attacks. As a result, on 13 Adar, five hundred attackers and Haman's ten sons, at the request of Esther, were hung on the gallows in Shushan, followed by a Jewish slaughter of seventy-five thousand Persians, although they took no plunder. Mordechai assumes a prominent position in Ahasuerus' court, and institutes an annual commemoration of the delivery of the Jewish people from annihilation.

Because of the bravery of Queen Esther, the Jews had "light, and gladness, and joy, and honor. And in every province, and in every city, wherever the King's commandment and his decree came, the Jews had joy and gladness, a feast and a good day. Many of the people of the land became Jews; for the fear of the Jews fell upon them." (Esther 8:1-17)

I am sure many of you are familiar with or have heard of the movie, "One Night With the King". It is the glorified film version of the story you have just read about Esther, a poor orphan girl who was taken in by her uncle, and his son Mordecai. This story is quite an attestation to what having the love of someone, and their beliefs in you can do. Although it is not highly likely (but not impossible with God) that you will become a Queen as your part in kingdom building, but you surely can be the best that you can be. Take the example from Esther, you *can* soar into higher heights if you only stretch out on your faith, and believe that God can . . . and God will!

Esther's royal position was no accident. She was put in a position of such great influence for a very specific purpose. Your position in life is no accident either. What can you envision that God might have for you to do right where you are, right now?

Mary: Blessed and Highly Favored Among Women ((Luke 1:27-28)

MARY. IN HEBREW: MIRIAM. MARY was the wife of Joseph and the mother of Jesus Christ, who was conceived within her by the Holy Spirit when she was a virgin. She is often called the "Virgin Mary," although never in scriptures are those two words put together as a proper name. The New Testament tells little of Mary's early history. Her parents are not named in the canonical New Testament; however, Church tradition and early non-biblical writings name her parents as Joachim and Anne. Her genealogy is given in Luke 3. She was of the tribe of Judah and the lineage of David (Psalm 132:11; Luke 1:32). She was connected by marriage with Elisabeth, who was of the lineage of Aaron (Luke 1:36).

While Mary resided at Nazareth with her parents (it is assumed), before she became the wife of Joseph, the angel of the Lord Gabriel came to her and announced that she was to be the mother of the promised Messiah (Luke 1:35-38). Mary cowered in fear and amazement when Gabriel appeared which was not an uncommon reaction. More often than not, in all of the scriptures where an angel appeared to a human being, the reaction was fear. We are not given an exact description of what an angel looks like, but Matthew says the angel's "countenance was like lightening, and his raiment (clothes) were white as snow; and for fear of the angel, the grave keepers did shake (trembled) and became as dead men (fainted)." (Matthew

28:3-4) Since angels are supernatural beings, it is obvious from the reactions of those who see them, they are therefore frightening. How even more frightened Mary must have been when the angel told her she was going to have a child, even though she had never had sex before in her young life! How could she tell her soon to be husband she was pregnant? What would he think of her?

Although she accepted what the angel told her as good news, Mary was still stunned, and retreated to visit her cousin Elisabeth, who was living with her husband, Zacharias, in the city of Juda, a considerable distance of about 100 miles from Nazareth. Immediately on entering the house she was saluted by Elisabeth as 'the mother of her Lord', and said to Mary, "blessed art thou among women, and blessed is the fruit of thy womb." So Elisabeth counseled with Mary as she pondered the things that were in her heart, and she remained in the home of Elisabeth and Zacharias for three months; then Mary returned to Nazareth to her own home. (Luke 1:46-56)

In the meantime, Joseph was supernaturally made aware of her condition in a dream, and instead of putting Mary away privately which was his first instinct, he took her into his own home. But imagine Joseph when he first heard the rumors that Mary was pregnant. How hurt and disappointed he was! He had to be a God fearing man to accept the explanation the angel gave him in the dream. (Matt. 1:18-25) How do you think you would have reacted? What would you have really thought in your mind?

Soon after this, the decree of Augustus was made that all the world should be taxed, everyone into his own city of residence. This required that they should proceed to Bethlehem some 80 or 90 miles from Nazareth; and while they were there, Mary went into labor. Joseph tried to find shelter in an inn or khan provided for strangers, but, as the inn was crowded, Mary had to retire to a place among the cattle, and there she brought forth her son, who was called Jesus because he was to save his people from their sins. (Luke 2:1-7)

This was followed by the presentation to Simeon and Anna in the temple, the flight into Egypt, and their return in the following year, to take residence at Nazareth. There for thirty years Mary, the wife of Joseph the carpenter, resides, filling her own humble sphere, and pondering over the strange things that had happened to her. (Matt. 2). During these years only one event in the history of Jesus is recorded: His going up to Jerusalem when twelve years of age, and his being found among the doctors in the temple (Luke 2:41-52). Probably also during this period Joseph died, for he was not mentioned again.

After the commencement of our Lord's public ministry, little notice is taken of Mary. She was present at the marriage in Cana. A year and a half after this we find her at Capernaum (Matt. 12:46-49), where Christ uttered the memorable words, "Who is my mother? and who are my brethren? And he stretched forth his hand toward his disciples, and said, Behold my mother and my brethren!" The next time we find her is at the cross along with her sister Mary (wife of Cleophus), and Mary Magdalene, and Salome, and other women. (John 19:26). From that hour John took her to his own abode. She was with the little company in the upper room after the Ascension (Acts 1:14). From this time she totally disappears from public notice. The time and manner of her death are unknown. Mary's other sons included Joses (Joseph), James, Judas (Juda), and Simon. There were evidently sisters as well, but they are unnamed (Matthew 13:55-56; Mark 6:3).

What a life for Mary! . . . Blessed among women!? . . . It is quite clear, that women during Mary's time, was still under the obscurity of men, and still definitely not recognized as a viable part of society, so much so, that *all* of Mary's sons are named in the Word, but *none* of her daughters are even named. From the ridicule of "pregnant at the tender age of about 12 or 13 years old . . . out of wedlock . . . and her fiancé is not even the father!" On the run right after the baby Jesus is born (flight into Egypt) . . . no respect when their family finally returns to Nazareth . . . and the list go on up to the agony of having to see your child being murdered on the cross in public humiliation, 'paying a debt He did not owe, because we owed a debt we could not pay'!

Can you say "overcoming", "brave", "humble", "faithful"?? All of these words are used to describe Mary, the mother of our Lord and Savior Jesus Christ. Yes, she was definitely blessed among women and highly favored by God to be allowed to be the vessel used to bring our savior into the world.

The most significant woman in Jesus' life was, of course, Mary, His mother. She remained in the background during His years of public ministry, perhaps caring for her younger children and/or grandchildren. Jesus portrayed gentle care of His mother while He was hanging on the cross, revealing a son's true love for his mother. It can indeed be taken as acceptable 'validation' of the importance of women from the Master Himself.

Women of God, in order for God to use us in His kingdom building, we must truly be those things named above and even more! Can those words that describe Mary be used to describe YOU?

EXAMPLE #8

Mary Magdalene: Delivered From Demonic Oppression (Luke 8:2)

Mary Magdalene was of the district of Magdala, on the shores of the Sea of Galilee, where stood her families castle, called Magdalon; she was the sister of Lazarus and of Martha, and they were the children of parents who were reputed noble, or, as some say, royal descendants of the House of David. On the death of their father, Syrus, they inherited vast riches and possessions in land, which were equally divided between them.

Mary Magdalene is described, in the New Testament, as one of the most important women in the movement of Jesus throughout his ministry. The late 20th and early 21st centuries have seen a restoration of the figure of Mary Magdalene, as a patron of women's preaching and ministry. Her new popularity has stemmed in part from the recognition that Mary Magdalene has suffered from what some believe to have been a historical defamation of character. She has been thought to be, in historical tradition, misidentified as a repentant prostitute, and depicted in art as a weeping sinner wiping Jesus' feet with her hair. Some New Testament scholarship has shown that this picture of Mary Magdalene is not true.

According to Luke 8:2 and Mark 16:9, Jesus cleansed her of "seven demons," a concept usually associated in the New Testament with healing from illness, not forgiveness of sin. Mary Magdalene is the leader of a group of women disciples who are present at the cross, when the male disciples (excepting John the Beloved) have fled, and at his burial site. Mary was a devoted follower of Jesus, entering into the close circle of those taught by Jesus during his Galilean ministry. She became prominent during the last days, accompanying Jesus during his travels and following him to the end. She witnessed his Crucifixion and burial. According to all four Gospels in the Christian New Testament, she was the first person to see the resurrected Christ.

Mary Magdalene is referred to in early Christian writings as "the apostle to the apostles." In apocryphal texts, she is portrayed as a visionary and leader of the early movement, who was loved by Jesus more than the other disciples. Several Gnostic gospels, such as the Gospel of Mary, written in the early second century, see Mary as the special disciple of Jesus who has a deeper understanding of his teachings and is asked to impart this to the other disciples. In all four gospels, Mary Magdalene is first witness to the Resurrection. John 20:16 and Mark 16:9 both straightforwardly say that Jesus' first post-resurrection appearance was to Mary Magdalene alone. Mary's role as a witness is unusual because women at that time were not considered credible witnesses in legal proceedings.

(Frank Stagg, Ph.D. (1911-2001), noted Southern Baptist Theologian, Seminary Professor, Author, Pastor)

Because of this, and because of extra-biblical traditions about her subsequent missionary activity in spreading the Gospel, the title "Equal of the Apostles" has been given to her. In Matthew 28:9, Mary Magdalene is with the other women returning from the empty tomb when they all see the first appearance of Jesus. In Luke 24 the resurrection is announced to the women at the tomb by "two men in clothes that gleamed like lightning" who suddenly appeared next to them. The first actual appearance by Jesus that Luke mentions is later that day, when Cleopas and an unnamed disciple walked with a fellow traveler they later realized was Jesus. Mark 16 describes the same appearance as happening after the private appearance to Mary Magdalene. The gospels of Mark and Luke record that the rest of the disciples did not believe Mary's report of what she saw, and neither Mary Magdalene, nor any of the other women, are mentioned by name in Paul's catalog of appearances at ; 1 Corinthians 15. Instead, Paul writes that Jesus "appeared to Peter, and then to the Twelve". Indeed, after her disbelieved first report of a resurrection vision, Mary Magdalene disappears from the New Testament. The "Acts of the Apostles" does not mention her (A title bestowed as a recognition of a saints' outstanding service in the spreading and assertion of Christianity, comparable to that of the original apostles), and her fate remains undocumented scripturally.

Mary Magdalene, a woman possessed by seven demons, was restored to her right mind; her bondage became a thing of the past. People around her marveled at the change that took place in her. How could she not love and trust such a man as Jesus Christ, who saved her? She became close to Jesus, witnessing healing after healing by Him. She was refreshed and renewed by His teachings. How could she *not* want to do everything for Him? Can you overcome all your life trials and yet remain loving and faithful to the Lord? Or do you feel sorry for yourself and remain unproductive in your work for the kingdom?

When Jesus first appeared after his death, burial, and resurrection, it was NOT to rulers, kings, nor even to His chosen male disciples; but it was to a woman whose love had held her at the cross and led her to His grave. Mary Magdalene, a person who had been afflicted by demons, whose testimony would not have held up in court just because she was a *woman* . . . was Jesus' first witness of the Resurrection! Once again, God had revealed himself to the lowly, and it would only be the humble whose hearing was sharp enough to perceive the message of His love.

In New Testament times, most women spent the majority of their time and energy within their homes, caring for their families. Mary Magdalene was one of the few women who dared step outside the cultural expectations of their time, to play a significant role in the ministry of Jesus. These women even used their own financial resources to support Jesus and His disciples. They purchased and prepared food for them, then served it as needed. They found homes and provided places for them to stay while on the road in ministry. Some women who either had no children or family, or perhaps their children were grown, had time to provide for the needs of Jesus and His disciples. Are YOU such a woman? How much of your time and finances do you give to the Lord in kingdom building? How do you fit the things of the Lord into your 'busy schedule'? . . . Do you even make time for Him?

The gospel of Luke in particular portrays Jesus as someone who both understood and respected women, conferring on them a stature that most of them had never enjoyed. Jesus' dealings with women throughout the gospels give all of us, men and women alike, a true and real model to follow as we consider the status and treatment of the women with whom we come into contact every day.

EXAMPLE #9

<u>Deborah</u>: Prophetess, Judge, Warrior, Saved (Judges 4-5)

DEBORAH OR DEBRA (HEBREW: "HONEY BEE") was a prophetess and the fourth, and the only female, Judge of pre-monarchic Israel in the Old Testament. Her story is told twice, in chapters 4 and 5 of Judges. Judges 5 gives this same story in poetic form. This passage, often called The Song of Deborah, may date to as early as the 8th century BCE and is perhaps the earliest sample of Hebrew poetry. It is also significant because it is one of the oldest passages that portray fighting women, the account being that of Jael, the wife of Heber, a Kenite tent maker. Jael killed Sisera by driving a tent peg through his temple as he slept. The account is interesting in that both Deborah and Jael are portrayed as strong independent women. The poem may have been included in the Book of the Wars of the Lord. (Numbers 21:14)

Little is known about Deborah's personal life. In the Book of Judges, it is stated that she was the wife of Lappidoth (meaning "torches"). But since this name is not found outside of the Book of Judges, it might simply mean that Deborah herself was a "fiery" spirit. She was powerful and she rendered her judgments beneath a palm tree between Bethel in the land of Ephraim, and Ramah in Benjamin. (Judges 4:5) Some people today refer to Deborah as the mother of Israel because of the "Song of Deborah and Barak". (Judges 5)

After being oppressed by Jabin, the king of Canaan, in Hazor, for twenty years, (Judges 4:9) Deborah prevailed upon Barak to face Sisera, the commander of Jabin's army, in battle. The victory to which the Bible refers is the victory of an Israelite force of ten thousand over Sisera's force of nine hundred iron chariots. Barak agreed to the battle only after Deborah agreed to accompany him into battle. recounts Deborah's assent to Barak's request:

> "And she said, I will surely go with thee: notwithstanding the journey that you take shall not be for your honor; for the LORD shall sell Sisera into the hand of a woman. And Deborah arose, and went with Barak to Kadesh." (Judges 4:9-10)

According to the Biblical account, the Israelites went out to meet the army of Sisera in battle. When Deborah saw the army, she said, according to Judges 4:14:"Up; for this is the day in which the LORD hath delivered Sisera into your hand: is not the LORD gone out before thee? So Barak went down from Mount Tabor, and ten thousand men after him."

Most of the then Egyptian territory was up in arms and there were few allies among the southern tribes who were free to come to the assistance of Deborah and Barak. Israel, which the song of Deborah and Barak numbers at 40,000 spears, was unavailable except for forces from the tribes of Ephraim, Benjamin, Machir, Zebulon, Issachar, and Naphtali. As Deborah's forces moved down from Kadesh in the mountains, the enemy moved north, taking the southern route up to Megiddo where the battle was fought. With 900 iron-bound chariots involved on either side, it was clearly a sizable battle, likely to be historically recorded by both sides. It can't be the account of the historical Battle of Megiddo given by Thutmoses III, around 1470 BCE, but it does agree with the taking of the narrow mountain road that was more susceptible to ambush and thus arriving with the advantage of surprise; and in the fact that the king of Kadesh was involved in the battle.

As Deborah prophesied, the Lord gave the victory to the Israelites. The Egyptian leader, Sisera, fled the battle site seeking refuge in the tent of the woman Jael. In the Biblical account, Jael killed the enemy leader, Sisera. After the battle, there was peace in the land for forty years. (Judges 5)

Deborah's vision of the world was shaped not by the political situations of her day, but by her relationship with God. Though women in the ancient world did not usually become political leaders, Deborah was just the leader that Israel needed: A prophetess who heard God and believed Him, whose courage aroused the people thus enabling them to throw off their foreign oppression. Deborah's people had sunk into despair because of their idolatry, forgetting God's promises and the faith of their ancestors. However, the fact that God turned the enemy's strength on its head, bestowing power to the weak and blessing Israel with peace for forty years, is just another attribute to the statement: "God uses whom He chooses in any way H sees fit to do so."

Deborah has been an encouragement to women throughout the years. Whenever women feel confined or mistreated, or if they are unsure of what is right or which way to proceed, when entering unknown territory; when they feel overlooked or ignored... women can always gain stability and help from remembering the story of Deborah.

Whatever Deborah had back then, is available to you, Women of God, today... right now! Her wisdom, her bravery, her confidence in God, her inner strength, her leadership qualities, can ALL be obtained by YOU. It comes from a true relationship with God, a complete trust only in God, and your willingness to be used by God however He chooses!

EXAMPLE #10

Tamar: Daughter of A King, Yet Helpless (II Samuel 13:14)

Tamar is a female name of Hebrew origin, meaning "date" (the edible kind), "date palm" or just "palm tree". There are two characters in the Bible with this name. Variants include "Tamara" and "Tamera". The name was not often used in traditional Jewish societies, possibly because both Biblical characters bearing the name are depicted as involved in controversial sexual affairs.

Tamar is a character in II Samuel in the Hebrew Bible. She was King David's daughter and the sister of Absalom. Her mother was Maacah, daughter of Talmai, king of Geshur. According to II Samuel 13:18, Tamar had a "richly ornamented robe" (NIV). Writers have connected this to Joseph's "Coat of Many Colors", and concludes that Tamar was a priestess, healer and "mistress of dreams".

According to the narrative in II Samuel 13, King David had a son, Absalom, who had a beautiful sister, Tamar, and King David had another son, Amnon, who professed to be in love with Tamar. Amnon was so obsessed with her, until his thoughts made him sick. Tamar was a virgin, and Amnon could not find any time alone with her. He had a good friend by the name of Jonadab (the son of David's brother Shimeah) who noticed that Amnon looked sad day after day, so he asked him what was wrong. Amnon confided in the very clever Jonadab, "I'm in love with Tamar, the sister of my half-brother, Absalom." Jonadab had a plan. He told Amnon, "You go to bed and pretend to be sick. When your father King David comes to see about you, beg of him to please let your sister Tamar come in to your room to cook for you so you can see her while she is cooking, and then she could feed him from her own hands."

So Amnon did as Jonadab, his cousin, had told him to do. He pretended to be sick, and when the King, his father sure enough came to see about him, he told the king what Jonadab suggested. His father David then sent for Tamar who was home in the palace and asked her to come to her brother Amnon who was sick, and prepare food in his presence. When Tamar arrived at the house, she began to cook food in the room where Amnon could watch her from his bed. But when she served the food, Amnon would not eat it. He told Tamar, "Have everyone else leave out, and then you bring the food to my bed so I can eat from your hands." When everyone was gone, Tamar brought the food to his bed, and when she tried to feed him, Amnon grabbed her saying, "Come lay with me my sister."

When Tamar objected saying, "No my brother. Don't force me. This is a disgraceful thing to do, and where could I live peaceably with the shame? And you, you would be out on the streets in disgrace. You know you can ask the king for my hand in marriage, and he would not withhold me from you." But Amnon would not listen, and being much stronger than Tamar, he raped her.

When it was over, Amnon hated her, even more than he had loved her before it all happened. So he told her to "Get up and leave!" But Tamar said, "No indeed! Sending me away is worst than what you just did to me." So Amnon called for his servant and told him, "Get this woman out of here away from me, and lock the door behind her." Now Tamar had worn her robe of many colors, which was in the tradition of the King's daughters who were virgins. She ran away crying bitterly, tearing off her robe and put ashes on her head. When Absalom found her, he asked her had Amnon forced her to have sex with him? Then Absalom said she should "Keep quiet about it. My sister. Amnon is your half-brother, and this should remain a family matter. Don't take it so hard to your heart." Then

Absalom had Tamar come live with him, where she remained sad, desolate, and alone. (II Samuel 13:1-20)

When King David, the father of Tamar, Amnon, and Absalom, heard the whole story about what had happened with Tamar and Amnon, he was very angry . . . but he did nothing to discipline Amnon, nor avenge or console Tamar. This made Absalom upset in his heart, and very enraged. He knew that their father favored Amnon because he was his firstborn. So Absalom stopped speaking to Amnon all together, because he hated him for raping his sister Tamar. (II Samuel 13:2122)

As the story unfolds, Absalom could not forget what his brother Amnon had done to their sister, Tamar, and continued to plot how he may avenge her. Some two years passed, and he eventually did actually kill Amnon for the rape of his sister. Absalom fled to Geshur and hid there for three years. (II Samuel 13:23-38)

Tamar's life was ruined. She had pleaded with Amnon to "not do this", a plea that has echoed over the centuries by women who have been victims of rape. God's reaction to sexual sin is quite evident throughout the Bible. He does not turn away from the victim, nor does he allow the rapist to go unpunished! (Deuteronomy 22: 25-27)

This was a tragic "family mess" at its finest!. Tamar, the daughter and sister was raped. One son and brother, Amnon, fell victim to his own lust and committed the rape of his own sister. The other son and brother, Absalom, felt his sister's pain, abhorred his father the king's apathy, and loathed his brother's action of rape so badly that he was driven to hatred strong enough to make him kill his own brother. But if you think about it, they ALL kept it a secret . . . even the victim! Was it that they were 'family', and did so out of some kind of sick 'loyalty'??

The Bible does not overlook the fact, nor glory in it that God's people participated in these dread acts. It clearly describes many instances of rape, incest, homosexuality, and adultery. Now, why would a Holy God think it necessary to include such sordid stories in the scriptures for His children?? . . . I'm glad you asked! . . .

Perhaps it is because He knows our thoughts, actions, lusts, and other weaknesses, . . . even if the world is blind to them! We may hide our actions from each other, but we can't hide them from God.

It is through these stories that God reminds us that He never forsakes His own, whether victim or criminal. Just as He offers help and comfort to the victims, never forsaking them in their trouble, He also offers healing and forgiveness to the evildoers.

So get ready, Women of God, AKA kingdom builders! No matter what you have experienced in life, it can be used to further your efforts in discovering your part in kingdom building. It does not matter whether you have been to the mountain top or the valley low. It does not matter whether you have always had the love and support of family and friends or grew up an orphan with no one in life to nurture or care for you. It does not matter whether you have notoriety and accolades of a king or queen, or you are just another fish in the sea and no one knows who you are and what you do. It does not matter whether you have been saved for sixty years or sixty minutes . . . or not yet! Make no mistake . . . every one who is in the Kingdom of God has a divinely planned part to complete in the Kingdom. The thing to do now is to ask yourself: "Am I truly in the Kingdom of God, and what are His plans for me?"

OUR DAILY PRAYER

"HEAVENLY FATHER, I WANT TO HEAR your voice. Help me to recognize and resist all the phony voices and enable me to distinguish yours from all the others. Make me a woman who both listens to and speaks your word. Help me surrender my darkness to you, and please flood me with the light of your presence. Help me, Dear Lord, to not lament my past; help me focus on my present; and help me to just know that my future is all in your hands. I am trusting in you to give me what I need, when I need it, where I need it, and the knowledge of how best to use it when I get it. All in Jesus' name, I submit this petition to you. Amen."

BIBLIOGRAPHY

King James Version, The Holy Bible.

Lucado, Max (1995) The Inspirational Study Bible (NKJV), Life Lessons from the Inspired Word of God

MacArthur, John (2006) Twelve Extraordinary Women Workbook, How God Shaped Women of the Bible and What He Wants to Do with You

Nelson, Thomas (2006) The Parallel Study Bible, (NKJV), (NCV), The Message, and Comprehensive Study Notes

Spangler, Ann & Jean E. Syswerda (1999) Women of the Bible, A One-Year Devotional Study of Women in Scripture

www.ingramcontent.com/pod-product-compliance
Lightning Source LLC
Chambersburg PA
CBHW020548080526
44583CB00013B/1055